THE CONSOLATION OF GARDENS

THE CONSOLATION OF GARDENS

by Diane Marquart Moore

Photography by Victoria I. Sullivan

Copyright © 2019 Diane Marquart Moore

Border Press
PO Box 3124
Sewanee, Tennessee 37375
www.borderpressbooks.com
borderpress@gmail.com

All rights reserved. No part of this book may be used in any manner without written permission.

ISBN: 978-0-9997804-6-6

Library of Congress Control Number: 2019942492

Cover: *Spring Annunciation* by Karen Bourque

Cover design by Martin W. Romero

Book design by Victoria I. Sullivan

Printed in the United States

For my grandchildren and great-grandchildren hoping they will always find consolation in gardens.

I perhaps owe having become a painter to flowers.
— Claude Monet —

TABLE OF CONTENTS

Half-Title i
Title iii
Copyright iv
Dedication vii
Epigram ix
Table of Contents xi
List of Images xv
New Poems 1
    Waiting for Spring on the Mountain 3
    Ora Et Labora 7
    A Thief in the Garden 9
    Morning Meditation 11
    Miniature Garden 13
    The Garden of Gethsemane 17
    The Gardens of Dora and Dicey 19
    In the Garden Alone 23
    The Garden of Melli Rah 27
    Gourd Garden 31
    Victory Garden Revisited 35
    Vegetable or Flower 39
    Among the Mayapples 43
    Garden Statue 47
    Radiant Faces 49
    Guardian Angels 53
    Vickie, the Indoor Gardener 57
    Trillium 61
    The Lilies of the Field 65
        II 67
    Feed My Geese 69
    Drawings of Dorothy Greenlaw Marquart 71

Selections From "The Road to Pineville" ... 73
   The Road to Pineville ... 77
      II ... 79
      III ... 81
      IV ... 83
      V ... 85
      VI ... 87
      VII ... 89
Acknowledgements ... 91
Author Biographies ... 93

LIST OF IMAGES

Three daffodils from home garden, Sewanee, Tennessee 3
Ora et Labora, Convent of St. Mary, Sewanee, Tennessee 6
St. Francis statue in garden, Sewanee, Tennessee 8
Cedar trees in yard, New Iberia, Louisiana 10
Succulents in home in Sewanee, Tennessee 13
Red roses 19
Saguaro from postcard 22
Roses on University of the South campus, Sewanee, Tennessee 27
Gourds in yard, Sewanee, Tennessee 31
Victory Garden, official US poster 35
Pansy in garden, Sewanee, Tennessee 39
Mayapple, University of the South, Sewanee, Tennessee 43
Sunflower by Janet Faulk-Gonzales, Broussard, Louisiana 49
Willow along Goat Mountain Trail, Sewanee, Tennessee 53
Jack-in-the Pulpit in woods, Sewanee, Tennessee 57
Trillium in Huntsville Botanical Garden, Huntsville, Alabama 61
Collage of flowers from home yard, Sewanee, Tennessee 64
Sketches by Dorothy Greenlaw Marquart 70

NEW POEMS

WAITING FOR SPRING ON THE MOUNTAIN

When the wren returns to nest
under the eaves of our porch

I will know spring has returned
and I am home

'though winter holds fast…
Daffodils, fading yellow in the woods,

wither under news of dying friends,
an oblivion replaced by insects

looking through blurred windows
singing of a season passing.

My herb garden
has overwintered in defiance

and on a table in the living room
a metal dragonfly flies into yellow pollen,

the forest waiting
for misshapen branches to move,

leaf out green
with the patience of an old lover.

ORA ET LABORA

The Sisters planted lavender in a neglected field,
working consecrated earth for female survivors:
women no longer in bondage to abuse,
addiction, violence in the streets,
evidence of damages in prostitutes
who had worn short skirts and boots —
maybe even a tattered fur piece —
composites of used up body parts
bled of something higher up.

It was a field of harvested goodness
the Sisters sent to the survivors
who made the crop into scent for bottles,
tubes of hand lotion, soap,
shampoo purified by eager hands,
wickedness recycled to outlast dark histories.
Sisters picked lavender in the crucible of summer,
pausing only to dance barefoot between rows,
chanting their tribal psalms under noonday sun:

Thou art gracious unto thy land…
Come write thy love on our hearts.

A THIEF IN THE GARDEN

Sage, thyme, lavender remained
while we were away

but someone crossed garden perimeters,
stole a colored glass bluebird

and a glass cardinal I had placed
in the warmth of a driftwood nook.

The visitor hadn't dared to touch
St. Francis in his new brown robe,

and I knew it was someone
who needed the cheer of birds

to replace the sad ones
beating in his chest.

He had plundered them for a hard winter
spent alone in an abandoned house,

hadn't put up welcome signs at supper time
'though he had hoped someone would enter

his yard choked with tall weeds,
had come inside to claim

the radiant birds of cheer
flying out of shadows.

MORNING MEDITATION

Daffodils bleed yellow into white collars
like guilty children bending their heads,
an unintentional garden not planted by us.
In front of our cottage
a squirrel selects one mushroom
and scurries to an empty bird bath
to stand on its stone rim.
He is surrounded by iris,
eats rapidly, at first wary
of marauders hiding behind the fence,
his set-up endangered.
An old cedar stretches out its arms,
leaves shivering overhead,
sparrows in its branches silent.
The squirrel soon ignores his premonitions
about invasions, breakfast interruptions,
raises his tiny hands against a phantom
crossing the deserted yard,
continues to feast on the head
of the mushroom. A moment captured,
makes faces at his future —
theft by other early risers.

MINIATURE GARDEN

I thought it was a miniature garden,
Cacti the Amish woman sold me.

She had become an unfaithful follower
advanced in spirit from her origins

but afraid of icons, rosaries
the adoration of saints.

And the pot did not hold Cacti,
deceived me in appearance.

Still, a singular inspiration,
this tiny particle of good things seen.

Cacti are sticker trees,
I once told my oldest daughter —

*plants with dagger points —
look but don't touch.*

They thrive in places of cool nights
where you might see ghosts,

the mirage of phantoms
sleep walking when lights are out

and you go missing until daybreak.
It was only a small gray pot

abandoned to its own resources,
beauty to which the sun was drawn,

a pot filled with succulents shaped like roses
safe indoors, hiding from burning winds,

little flags of fading color, long suffering
but alive where all else dies.

THE GARDEN OF GETHSEMANE

The olive trees with their twisted trunks
became s site of agony frozen,
something perishing without peace,
the soul lost among their limbs,
sun draining above them.

A place of rest He often claimed
at the foot of Mount Olive,
garden of consolation become desolation,
olives gathered and pressed three times
He emulated in prayers of anxiety three times,

passing from the Garden of Eden — life —
into Gethsemane, Garden of death,
an ancient grove of inhuman figures,
the trees 900 years on earth,
and did He not deserve such longevity?

The immortality of sadness in that place
altered nothing, tears of blood
fell among the dismal trees
instructing the darkness,
speaking of love no one accepted.

THE GARDENS OF DORA AND DICEY

It was the age of walking through gardens —
afternoon entertainment, growing and showing,
arranging bouquets, the burden of hoe and weed
lost to Dora except for arrangements, table settings,
her roses in silver and crystal vases.

Theirs was a competition,
Dicey triumphing, Dora taking to her bed,
a room dense with fragrances of gardenias
Dicey brought her, the acrid scent of jealousy
hanging above Dora's canopied bed.

I remember Dora's fond looks at me,
the embrace of adopted motherhood,
flowers, the standard of her deep affection.
Then, my husband and I divorced
and she stopped gardening.

The efflorescences had been her competition…
and her acceptance of me.
Anger, she said, *is a bow to insanity*.
never mind jealousy,
her years of competition with Dicey.

She entered solitude without flowers,
weeds over blossoms her spite,
but Dicey's backyard flourished until death.
Dora's, to her husband's sometime tending.
She, the proud lover of endings.

IN THE GARDEN ALONE

When I saw her lying in the silver coffin,
sharp Greenlaw nose upturned,
wearing a dress with tiny red buttons,
I wept for abuses she had suffered,

and when the electronic organ began
"I Come to the Garden Alone,"
the shadow of her journey past
came alive with His Passion's wounds.

Flowers banked against the wall beside her
dropped their blossoms into my hands,
my recalcitrant father asking
like the imaginary gardener in John's Gospel:

Woman why are you weeping?

If she had favored that hymn,
her garden would have been different,
plants struggling to exist,
small leaves reducing transpiration,

desert plants she had seen
traveling to California and Diddy Wah Diddy:
the Crown of Christ thorn of spikes,
or a Night Blooming Cereus

blooming throughout one desert night,
not to open again for another year.
O Mother, you who loved sun and sand,
would that you had returned in a year

as the white crown of a Sahuaro
to live at least three years without rain
in a venerable garden, a living thing
He might have planted for the elf owl

who had come to the garden alone,
longing for his call to a death.

THE GARDEN IN MELLI RAH

An intransigent gardener waters
five rose bushes blooming yellow
against a blue sky without cloud,
ignoring Khuzestan's scarcity of water

while I sit tapping on a portable Olivetti,
resentful of water coming from the hose,
deprived of creeks, rivers, bayous…
only a calendar showing the River Amster.

Across a bridge spanning
the vigilant River Karun,
water as brown as the Bayou Teche,
flows into early spring.

The smell of oil and gas flares
smothers the scent of roses,
and beyond us in Ahwaz,
a city of half million gardeners

plant rose gardens inspired by Sadi's
Gulestan. Cyclamen, daisies,
poppies, oleander, and lale',
the wild tulip, also trapped in dry earth.

Here, seeds buried, then resurrected,
here, weeds border the gardens,
watching over clusters of heads
that crave awe, absorb suffering,

changing everything into sweetness,
gifts for moments that have been lost
pulsing like unprotected hearts,
red and visible.

GOURD GARDEN

Mother must have read an article;
(she was always saying:
"I read this article and…"),
and told my father that gourds
were sacred intermediaries

between the human and spiritual world.
It was an easy thing for her to believe —
being in the same realm as fairies,
ghosts, elves, anything supernatural.
She asked my abusive father

to plant a row…for him a likely step
from cucumbers, pumpkins,
all in the same family.
He got a book and read past
her short article and his abuse of her,

learning that the sacred seeds had floated
through the Atlantic to South Africa,
landed in Brazil and further
into the New World.
So he surrendered to her favor,

planted the seeds in March,
told her he knew everything
there was to know about gourds,
for her to be quiet and wait a year.
He had begun to believe these good omens

like the Africans, represented a woman's wealth.
(of which Mother had none or he had spent).
Together, they watched the hard-skinned ones
plump on the vines, drop at first frost
and he put them out to dry.

He hung his pleas for forgiveness
on a string suspended from the ceiling:
her idea of decor for a rotting screen porch,
seeds rattling within mottled brown objects
noisy with pardon he had exacted from her…

or so he thought.

VICTORY GARDEN REVISITED

I first wrote about the plot of patriotism
in rhyming verse, my introduction
to cocoa weed in a Victory Garden
luxuriant with new growth, circa 1943.

I was eight when I pulled those weeds,
pruning, unaware of tendrils
hiding a bee watching me labor
among rows of lettuce and radishes.

Sir Walter Raleigh tobacco in a red can
became balm from father's pipe,
pressed on stings to my forehead
by a Nazi bomber in a patriotic garden.

As an adult, confounded by tendrils
growing in a shower drain, El Paso, Texas,
I dared to pull them from their source
deep in the sands of a military base,

no victory garden, no lettuce beneath,
just some variant plant missing in action
from the parched desert life.
For us, a sign of encroaching poverty.

The U. S. Army, loving extremes,
sent us to northern Maine in winter,
growing ground of Irish potatoes,
frozen soil, November-May,

no weeds to pull, no bees humming,
dried pinto beans and king-size potatoes
weed-free wealth of body fat…
fulsome victory *without* a garden.

VEGETABLE OR FLOWER

Reports of more suicides came this morning
but later at retreat, a lecturer told us
the resurrection story of Lazarus,
how Martha, Mary, a cast of grieving characters

were called out of their despair
to witness a miracle, not a death or a suicide,
and I thought about Uncle George's miracle garden,
how gardening did not alter his irascible disposition
or call him out to resurrect a dying marriage.

Beans, tomatoes, sweet lettuce,
radishes, corn stalks formed a barrier
between his back porch and
his mother-in-law's sleeping porch next door.

She kept up her bed of pansies
and pink camellias, her hands
raw from working soil in spring.
He gave her produce for her supper;

She floated camellias in a silver bowl
for him. It was the best they could do
for a relationship, both fussy and critical,
gardens ameliorating their raspy voices.

They deserved the gardens,
days stretched long for both of them.
She, a widow with Bible her only companion,
he, a retired Navy man; his wife, secretary

for a judge whose company she preferred.
The gardeners were outdoors in good weather
as reliable as dark roast coffee at breakfast,
flowers centered on her kitchen table

his battered hoe hanging in the shed
until his wife's early departure for a job.
He could weed an entire field of vegetables
in a short morning and seldom suffered defeat

but nothing could change the fragile nature
of his lonely marriage and he knew
the old woman next door
had divined how it was to end things.

She had made a compromise with life
through her flower garden,
misdirected splendor, if ever…
but his table held plump tomatoes,

golden corn, greenest lettuce,
offerings from crumbled earth,
a gracious plenty, his wife said,
more providence than *she'd ever* wanted,
more miracle than she could allow.

AMONG THE MAYAPPLES

Climbing the hill that leads
from St. Mary's on a bright day,
the light became a gold stream descending
on a colony of mayapples.
I saw hiding among their umbrella leaves
a lone white flower

and a vision of my mother appeared
laughing through the shadow
of their upright leaves,
voiceless but full bodied,
dancing on an island of mingled love,
the white flower nodding absently at her.

I knew she was searching for elves
who would paint the yellow berries
yet to come, a place they had found
unheeding of tornado warnings and heavy rain,
the work of storms a part of every spring
arousing the gypsy spirit in her.

She disappeared without speaking
and I did not wonder why she had
come there from the *also world*
had looked down and made arrival plans
to dance among the mayapples,
to lift the stone from an unnoticed tomb,
seeing me lonely for places unknown.

GARDEN STATUE

St. Francis, his body photosynthesized
lime green, stands on a wet patio
clutching the Word
and reading to a bird at his feet.
His cloak only the South winds
showering catkins on his tonsured head
split by weather but not his notions of faith.
He is a green determination,
although he has lost his place,
unable to stuff his gown with newspaper
or ask someone to take him in.
He makes no attempt to kneel in prayer
like someone lately saved, born again,
waits for his discoloration to be seen,
for God to come along,
assure him he has a purpose,
will be the color of gray stone again,
returned to a park that looks for someone
who wants a steady job in the sun
and lives inside the soul.

RADIANT FACES

Van Gogh painted twelve radiant faces.
The sunflower is mine, he said,
his signature for five in Paris,
seven for the yellow house in Arles…
until the sun reclaimed their faces.

Janet planted a field of dazzling faces,
saying *the sunflower is mine,*
but slow to weed and water,
turn the earth around each stalk
their brown eyes closed against the sun.

The difference: Van Gogh captured brilliance,
canvas girdling the sun,
color setting and hardening
his dream of flooding light
caught in eternal splendor.

GUARDIAN ANGELS

Fingers of the willow
spread out along the shoreline,
know how to bend
in strange poses without snapping,
surrender to life.

Planets revolve around them
making no sound, winds whirl
and rain falls on their bent heads…,
Nature seeks reclamation.

Weather can wear away rock,
creating faces like aging humans
but the angel trees taunt mortality,
continue to bear seeds —

white cotton hair rushing out,
intrepid pilots and sailors
able to float in air and water —
seeds that plant themselves
to purify our doubts.

VICKIE, THE INDOOR GARDENER

She brings the garden to me,
gifts from a three-mile hike,
Goat Mountain Trail's natural park
or yards leading into the trail.
Her prize, Jack-in-the Pulpit,
who stands in his purple striped pulpit
waiting to deliver lofty sermons
about people who break off
his stem so he has to cease

mid-sentence pontifications
about a spirit unmoved by season.

In summer crimson berries appear
too late to announce the Passion,
and she says Jack seems to be
more like Jack-in-the Box
popping up, exciting her
to do the thing she likes most to do:
pinch plants and bring them home.
Now it has lived
in a small vase almost a week,
this prize plucked from a wildflower island
brought past the gates of natural habitat
by a plant poacher, unredeemed,
because she wants me to have a garden…
and has no desire to plant one.

TRILLIUM

Visions of them had come to me as I grasped the Pascal Candle at dawn, then processed indoors to the scent of Easter lilies, heavy with the memory of the Garden at Gethsemane. The air exhaled its last icy breath and beyond the altar, a colony of Trillium beckoned to me. The best places to find them were identified as a formal botanical garden, a national park, and rich hardwood slopes. I traveled to the formal garden and claimed a stone bench covered with lichen. There, I listened for the dialect of small flowers; they appeared to resemble infant angels chanting psalms of innocence: Lemon Toad Shade and neighboring Rainbow Wake Robin plants that emerged with the first robin song in spring. Nearby, a lost white bloom nestled in the root of a sweet gum, singular and unlabeled. Thousands of them had been collected, were on display beside a carnivorous plant bog, and I envisioned the seeds being carried away by ants doing their good work in a silent line dance. All of them needed the thing money could not buy: an audience of wonder and awe.

I. THE LILIES OF THE FIELD

The lawn tender will arrive today:
tractor, weeder without conscience,

blade and vigor mowing the field:
dandelion, fleabane, wild violets,

bugle weed — yellow, purple, white —
a garden of wildflowers at peak,

the only dispossessed lives I know
that exist in the bliss of Now.

"They do not toil, nor spin," *
these novitiates in brief pacts

with sunlight, long stalks incautious,
not trembling before losing their crowns

in a place of no argument,
leaving behind a wren building its nest

above a scarred meadow…
dying vessels of unconscious grace.

*from Jesus' *Sermon on the Mount*

II.

Even Adam the mower could not
fell the nation of bugleweed in the yard,
sparing the purple blooms here and there,
zealots in random clumps

like robins with unruffled feathers
still in the full flush of growing,
displaying tenderness in a harsh world,
heroic in the shadow of Adam's blade,

little purple plumes going on,
plants with a history of giving much
waiting to be taken down, unmindful
of the moment they have been.

FEED MY GEESE

I left the gardens and traveled to Pickwick Lake, and from the balcony of an inn I saw the long, black neck of a solitary Canadian goose bobbing, feeding on scant grass beneath my porch. She ignored me standing there above her and seemed impervious to the fact that she had abandoned her little ones at lake's edge. A man appeared, pulling a white dog on leash that coughed weakly, enough to send the mother goose flapping downhill, honking regret at betraying her lakeside offspring to search for her own substance of joy. The following morning, after rainfall, this mother mediatrix tried to make a dignified appearance, leading a flock of handsome geese and six little ones uphill, her moral failure forgiven by the docile family she had renounced, now following her… now sharing a banquet of wet grass.

I stood at the window of my room imagining her ruminating: *After all, she had just gone for a stroll. Years hadn't passed; the dog had been on a leash. The little ones could have made an exit into the lake alone. She couldn't cover their eyes forever. No feathers had flown, and they didn't live in a bird cage. She could have argued with herself further, but she saw the man sneaking out of the inn with the dog underarm — illegal entry; illegal exit. She had heard there was a fine for keeping an animal in rooms of the inn. She honked loudly, knowing she had witnessed human misdemeanor, then returned to feeding as the man climbed into the cab of a white pickup with the white dog and sped off. Well, breakfast was on the table. She helped herself to the tall grass and lost track of the little ones again. This predicament of parenting was too much for her. She waited to panic again, then remembered all of them had wings. Silly goose, searching her soul like a human.*

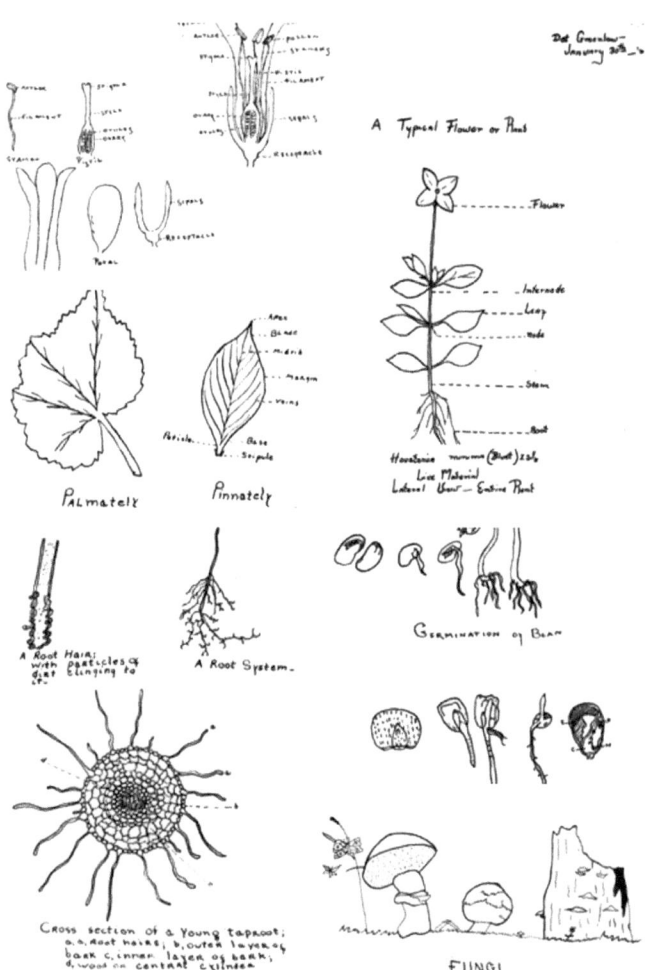

DRAWINGS BY DOROTHY GREENLAW MARQUART 1926

These drawings were rendered by my mother, Dorothy Greenlaw Marquart, who was a plant lover from the time of her adolescence in the 1920's until her death in 1978. As a Golden Eaglet Girl Scout during the 1920's, she showed an abiding interest in outdoor life and needed no goading to tell stories about camping in places like Juliette Low Camp in Alabama where she enjoyed wildlife and plant life to the fullest, often embellishing the experience with references to "a garter snake I kept in my bedroll," and describing the "thick forest" surrounding her camp site.

During Mother's senior year at Franklinton High School in Franklinton, Louisiana, she enrolled in a Biology Course that included a section on plant life, and at Mississippi Women's College (now defunct) in Hattiesburg, Mississippi, she majored in Art, but scheduled a course in Botany. I believe that she enrolled in the Botany course so she could create drawings of plants, and I am grateful that she preserved the two notebooks in which her drawings appeared.

Later, she painted pictures of gnomes, frogs, and plant life —oil paintings that disappeared from the family heirlooms, but I inherited the notebooks, scrapbooks, and postcards she treasured. I include these drawings because I think Mother (or "Momee," as we called her) sent a message for me to include her early work with plants in *The Consolation of Gardens*.

II. SELECTIONS FROM "THE ROAD TO PINEVILLE"

Afternoons in Oaxaca (Las Poesias), 1999

During 1998-99, when I trained to become an ordained deacon in the Episcopal Diocese of Western Louisiana, for nine months I traveled from my home in New Iberia, Louisiana to the Veteran's Hospital in Pineville, Louisiana and spent overnight stays in a large dormitory on the grounds of this hospital. The stay was a requirement for me to complete a unit of Clinical Pastoral Training, otherwise known in clergy lingo as "CPE." During my training I left my home in New Iberia, Louisiana before daylight, and two friends gave me gifts to assist me on my early morning travels: my first cell phone and a flashlight.

The two-hour trip afforded me an opportunity to greet the dawn on a stretch of countryside in which I saw very few cars and lots of plant life along the way. To break the monotony of the trip, I steered the car with my left hand and wrote lines of poetry in shorthand with my right hand, arriving at my destination with rough drafts of poems that would become part of *Afternoons in Oaxaca*, actually my first published volume of poetry.

I also added a section about my experiences with the people who were permanently confined to the hospital wards entitled "Ward Journal." The poems were written at night while I was on call in that large dormitory and could not sleep. Those poems are not included in this section of *The Consolation of Gardens*, but they were sent to a Clinical Pastoral Journal and were to appear in one of its issues that I've never seen.

The poems included here are probably the briefest of all the poetry I've published and were written under unsafe conditions while driving a car, but they seemed to beg for inclusion in *The Consolation of Gardens*.

Diane Marquart Moore
Sewanee, Tennessee
May, 2019

THE ROAD TO PINEVILLE

I.

The moon moves through mist
tinged with a stripe of blood.
Suspended above ancient trees
it hangs over a red barn slack with age
claiming landscapes like a jealous overlord,
a white and fading message in day-breaking sky:
I keep watch with you.

II.

At dawn, unseen birds gather,
squabbling about who will bless the day;
squads of palmettos appear
newly flooded by rain in the swamp.
I stop at the edge of brown water
and bless the dagger-like fans,
wild plants that have followed me
unabashed into the unknown…
like prayers spiking the underbrush.

III.

In fog inclined to cover the trees
early red buds break through to sunlight;
a veil overtaking the heart's desire
lifts to reveal unspoken devotion
not unlike spring's burst of purple.

IV.

Winter returns in the night
and tries to subvert the spring,

a lone white bird takes his stand on one leg
in a sea of buttercups whose faces,

upturned, catch an intrepid gust
without being swept away,

the natural world always altering its laws,
expecting us to stand fast.

V.

There is no unencumbered God.
Like a Bedouin he moves
across green fields,
searching out yellow cups,
columns of red clover,
unsettles a grackle diving at wandering egrets,
casts His shadow of the vigilant parent.

VI.

The grandfather thistle,
purple head and thorn,
leans top heavy
on a highway shore of weeds,
lures a dazed bee within
who ignores the thorn,
wings treading air,
nose-diving into seduction:
a warm sift of pollen,
radar awry, flight failed.

VII.

Traveling north, I remember the summer of childhood,
that time when I was always traveling toward green,
the tree-topped road leading to Grandmother and Grandfather.

When I arrived, new green greeted me:
a pear tree, the garden of cucumber and bean,
and I would look upward into a canopy,

the bower of love from Grandmother and Grandfather.
Everything seemed to be an everness of green
before Grandmother's hands bled raw with eczema

and Grandfather began to choke on his buttermilk.
The first winter with them turned brown and dry.
A shadow stood at the edge of the garden

the year I turned twelve and Grandfather died.
I still dream of him returning to life
although I am now past sixty.

That is how long deaths last,
how impermanent green is…

ACKNOWLEDGEMENTS

To Karen Bourque, glass artist, Church Point, Louisiana, for the lovely glass piece entitled *Spring Annunciation* that provided the cover photograph of *The Consolation of Gardens*;

Dr. Victoria I. Sullivan for her expert "camera eye" and resulting photographs, as well as design of book interior of this volume;

Martin Romero, Vice-President of Landscape Design for Mullin Landscape Associates, St. Rose, Louisiana, for cover design;

Darrell Bourque, Gary and Susan Entsminger, and Mary Ann Wilson for constant support of my writing;

The Sisters of St. Mary Convent, Sewanee, Tennessee for prayers and worship that feed The Muse.

POET

Diane Marquart Moore is a poet, journalist, book author, and blogger at *A Word's Worth*, who divides her time between Sewanee, Tennessee and New Iberia, Louisiana. She is a regular contributor to the Pinyon Review, has published in *The Southwestern Review at the University of Louisiana*, Lafayette, Louisiana, *Interdisciplinary Humanities*, *The Xavier Review*, *Acadiana Profile Magazine*, *American Weave*, *Louisiana Historical Review*, *Trace*, and other literary journals. She has been an Associate Editor for *Acadiana Lifestyle Magazine*, New Iberia, Louisiana, feature writer and columnist for *The Daily Iberian*, New Iberia, Louisiana, as well as a feature writer and book reviewer for T*he Yaddasht Haftegy* in Ahwaz, Iran where she lived during the reign of the Shahanshah. Her young adult book, *Martin's Quest*, was a finalist in the Heekins Foundation Award Contest and was selected to be on the supplementary reading list for gifted and talented students by the Louisiana Library Association. Moore is also a retired archdeacon of the Episcopal Diocese of Western Louisiana.

PHOTOGRAPHER

Victoria I. Sullivan is a writer, botanist, and photographer. She studied biology at the University of Miami, earned a Ph.D. in biology from Florida State University and held a faculty position in the Department of Biology at the University of Louisiana, Lafayette for 20 years. She has published poetry, flash fiction, many botanical papers and other nonfiction, two speculative fiction sequels, *Adoption* and *Rogue Genes*, and a book for nature enthusiasts, *Why Water Plants Don't Drown*. Sullivan is a resident of Sewanee, Tennessee, and winters in New Iberia, Louisiana.